GW00383831

BEST OF
GYM DESIGN

Imprint
The Deutsche Nationalbibliothek lists this publication in the Deutsche Nationalbibliografie;
detailed bibliographical data are available on the internet at http://dnb.d-nb.de.

ISBN 978-3-03768-046-9
© 2010 by Braun Publishing AG
www.braun-publishing.ch

The work is copyright protected. Any use outside of the close boundaries of the copyright
law, which has not been granted permission by the publisher, is unauthorized and liable
for prosecution. This especially applies to duplications, translations, microfilming, and any
saving or processing in electronic systems.

1st edition 2010

Project coordinator: Annika Schulz
Editorial staff: Jennifer Sandner, Rebecca Wrigley
Translation: Alice Bayandin
Graphic concept: Michaela Prinz

All of the information in this volume has been compiled to the best of the editors know-
ledge. It is based on the information provided to the publisher by the architects' and designers' offices and excludes any liability. The publisher assumes no responsibility for its
accuracy or completeness as well as copyright discrepancies and refers to the specified
sources (architects's and designers's offices). All rights to the photographs are property of
the persons / institutions state in the picture credits.

BEST OF
GYM DESIGN

move!

BRAUN

Preface

Dagmar Glück

Today, the conviction that fitness is a prerequisite for a true sense of personal well-being is more widespread than ever. Especially in urban areas, where outdoor sports are hardly possible, the desire for effective training bring people to fitness studios en masse. Buoyed by this global trend, the fitness industry is currently booming.

In addition to modern training devices and a comprehensive course range, more and more value is placed on fitness studio ambience, opening a new and exciting field of work for architects and interior decorators. "Move! Best of Gym Design" presents 42 creative and innovative examples of fitness design from around the world. The range stretches from wellness centers, classic fitness studios and exclusive hotel gym rooms to large-scale sport and recreation centers.

In the past, groaning, sweating musclemen pumped iron in threadbare warehouses, where air reeked of sweat and testosterone. The world of fitness has changed a lot since then. Fitness studios have long lost the grimy image of a weight room, and now target a discerning clientele. Today, weight training alone, without consideration for back pain and joints, is out of the question. Instead, holistic approaches that engage both mind and body are in demand. In a modern training program, concentration and relaxation have just as much importance as classic strength and endurance exercises. Asian traditions of body control have gained especially high acceptance, elevating yoga and meditation to a new significance. Since fitness

studios are often financed solely by their customers' monthly fees, price wars are regularly waged by big chains. A bare-walled hall, countless machines, mirrors, showers, and the low-budget fitness studio is complete. But not everyone feels comfortable and motivated to exercise in such an atmosphere. Modern studios offer customers an integrated wellness program in sophisticated surroundings, reflecting the new trend of combining fitness and wellness. Contrasted programs are brought together in one design, and thus weight and aerobics rooms are joined by relaxation rooms, meditation spaces and spas. The service range may be rounded out with a cosmetic studio, bistro or even child care.

This goal to combine movement and calm under one roof makes fitness design a special challenge for architects. The projects presented in this book show how power and relaxation can be fused together using color and light concepts and smart layout. Choice of materials plays a key role in creating the fitness room's ambience, and must take into consideration additional factors, such as vibrations from heavy training machines, moisture or chlorine. Air conditioning and ventilation are also of utmost importance, and even sound insulation may be an issue. For example, the Equinox Fitness Club in San Francisco is housed in a 1929 Art Deco building. STUDIOS Architecture succeeded in breathing new life into the generous, airy former trading hall. Its historical glass roof creates an open atmosphere for training and respiration. Relaxation zones for yoga, the spa, changing rooms and the pool are located in the basement.

Natural stone and warm wood dominate inside the Angelo Caroli Health Club in Milan. Paolo Colombo interpreted the demands of a modern training facility using clear lines and strict symmetry. Elegance and harmony emanate from the predominant forms and illumination; this is a space that brings soul and body into unison.

The design of the Aspria Spa + Sporting Club + Hotel in Berlin is a dialog with the building's aesthetics. The shell, reminiscent of industrial architecture, contains a soft, luxurious interior where fixtures remain clearly separate from the outer wall at all times. Simplified forms and the choice of refined materials such as palisander, natural stone and glass, as well as a differentiated color and illumination concept, all characterize the design by Bösl+Eck Architects and Heico Sönnichsen (spa).

Many fitness clubs attempt to attract as wide a customer base as they can; others present themselves as exclusive institutions. Some studios radiate a family atmosphere or offer fitness exclusively for women. On the other hand, gyms like the bodybuilder David Barton's studio chain want to attract young, hip party people in New York, Miami and Chicago. Here, training devices are ironically staged around an eerie-exquisite design as modern instruments of torture. On nights featuring top DJs, the studio turns into a nightclub.

Those taking up training in earnest must not only overcome their inner couch potato, but also have to stay on the ball, and this is where fitness design plays a definite role. Move! Shows just how dynamic architecture can be.

Angelo Caroli Health Club | Milan | Architetto Paolo Colombo

Warm earth colors and wooden elements stand in strong contrast with modern equipment.

Aspria Spa + Sporting Club + Hotel | Berlin | Bösl+Eck Architekten and Heico Sönnichsen (Spa)

Wellness and fitness in modern puristic design

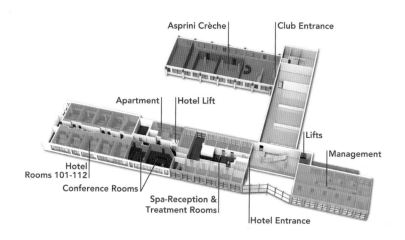

Asprini Crèche
Club Entrance
Apartment
Hotel Lift
Lifts
Management
Hotel
Rooms 101-112
Conference Rooms
Spa-Reception &
Treatment Rooms
Hotel Entrance

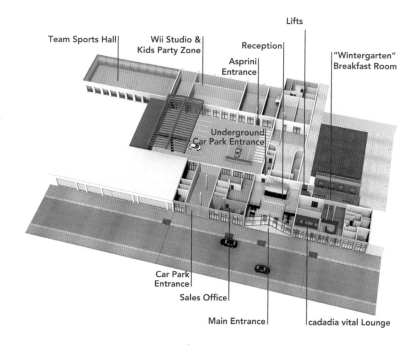

Team Sports Hall
Wii Studio &
Kids Party Zone
Lifts
Reception
Asprini
Entrance
"Wintergarten"
Breakfast Room
Underground
Car Park Entrance
Car Park
Entrance
Sales Office
Main Entrance
cadadia vital Lounge

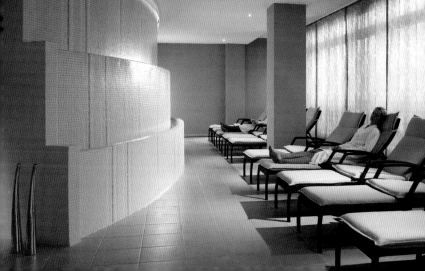

David Barton unveils a **40,000** square foot, **four-story fitness fantasy** in Astor Plac

Athens Holmes Place Health Club | Athens | Milner Associates Architects

S PLACE
H CLUB

There are many large surfaces such as wooden floors and solid dark oak walls, combined with specialized stainless steel and aluminum constructions

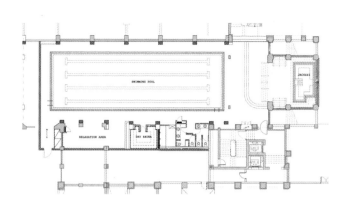

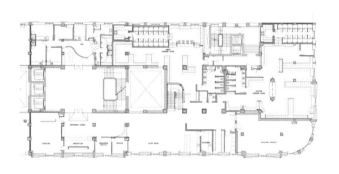

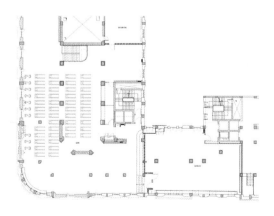

Azuolynas Sport Center I Kaunas I Vilius Ir Partneriai

The sport and health center is designed near open tennis courts in one of the most attractive parks of Kaunas

The most **vibrant colors** were used to **create** a memorable **image** of the place

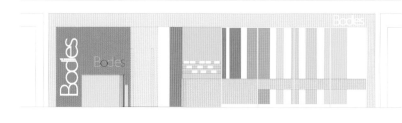

The **top-class fitness** and wellness **paradise** extends over a **4,000** square meter large area

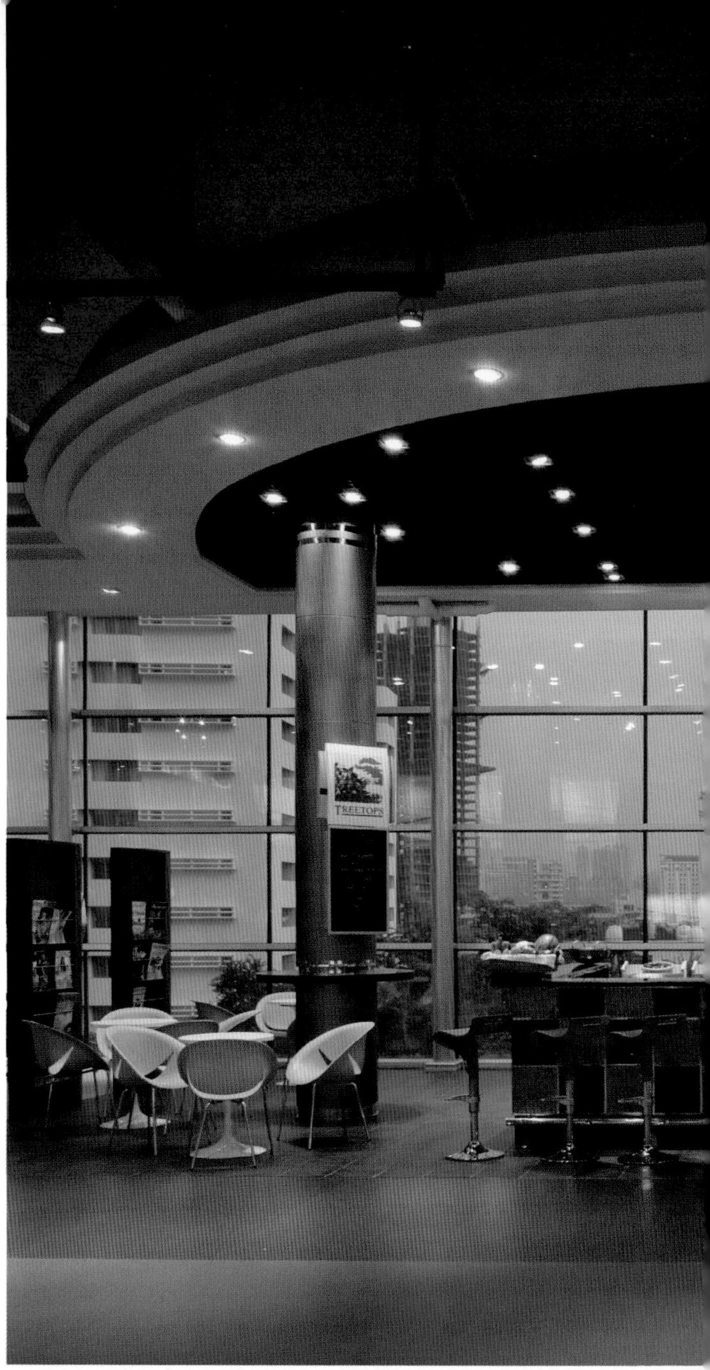
TREETOPS

A place where **individuals** can work at their **own pace** in a **fun** and **stylish** environment

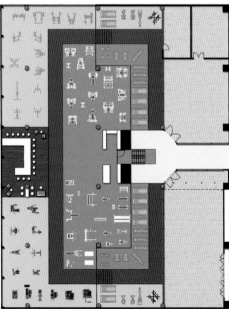

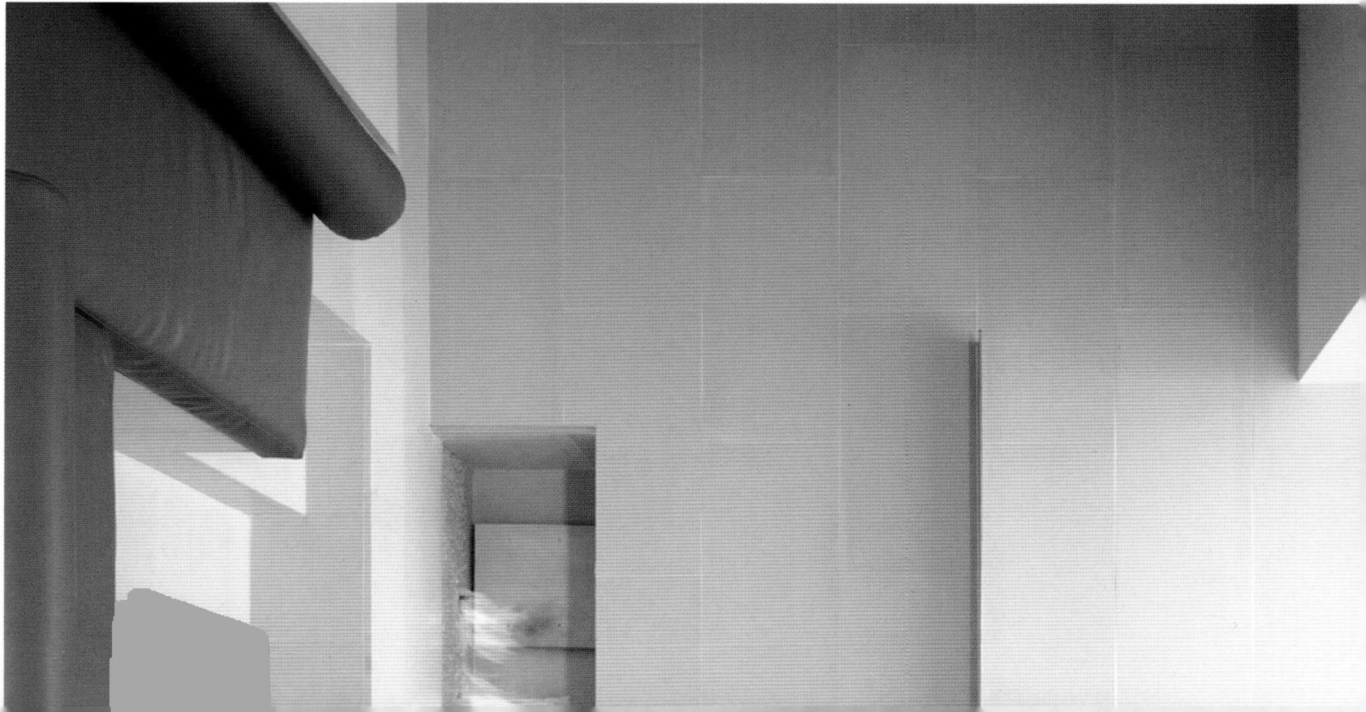

Light-colored Australian
floor tiles **cover** the
entire **central area**

The interior **should set** the visitors mind on sport **even** without pieces of **sports equipment**

Equinox Fitness | San Francisco | STUDIOS Architecture

This open, **airy space** provides an **inspiring** setting for long, **refreshing** exercise sessions

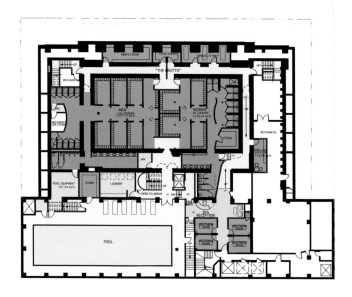

Soft pastels, organic shapes
and warm lights –
the interior design transmits
a feeling of safety and comfor

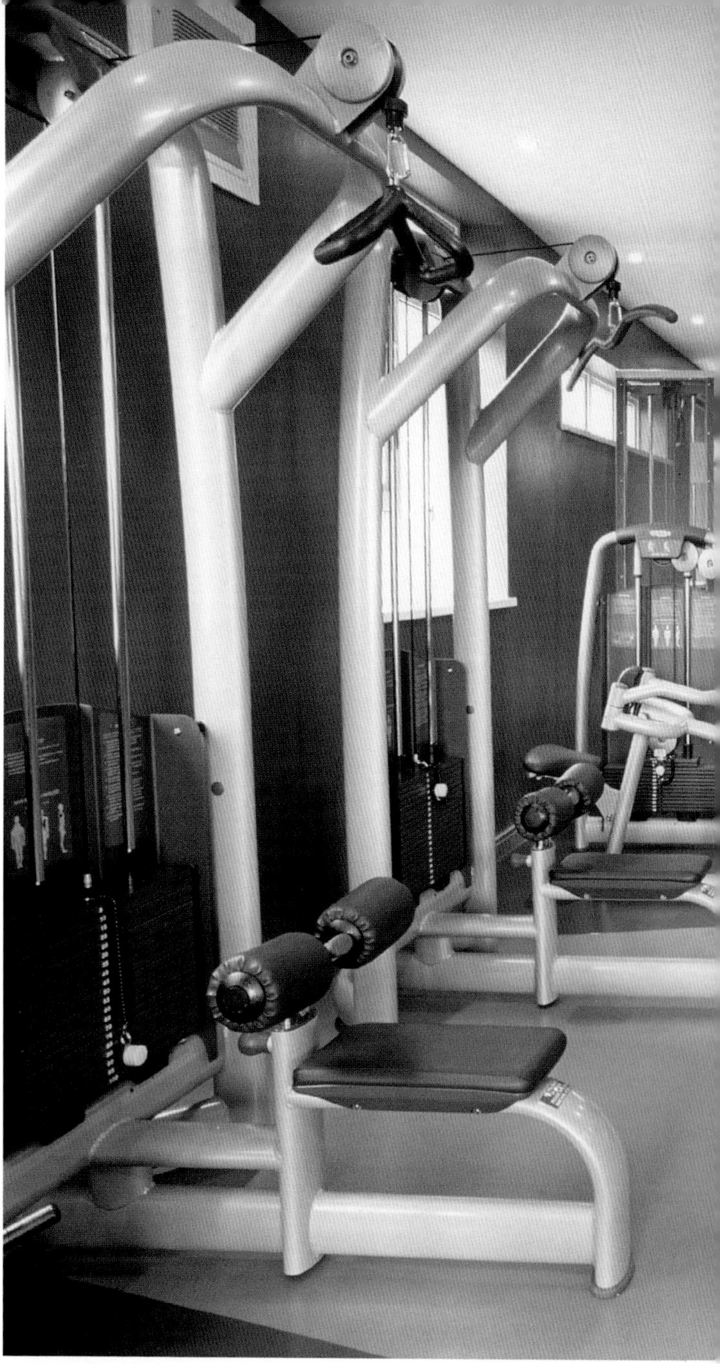

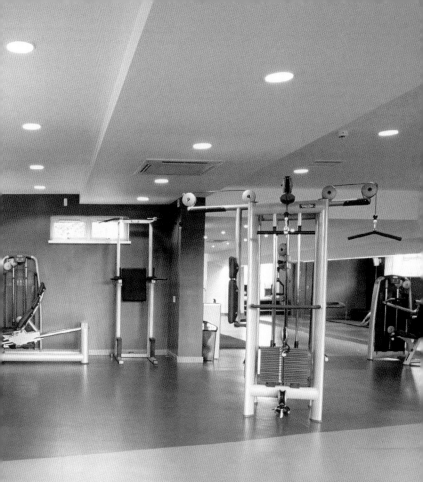

Different **shades of blue colorize** the fitness studio, giving it a touch of **coolness** and **modernity**

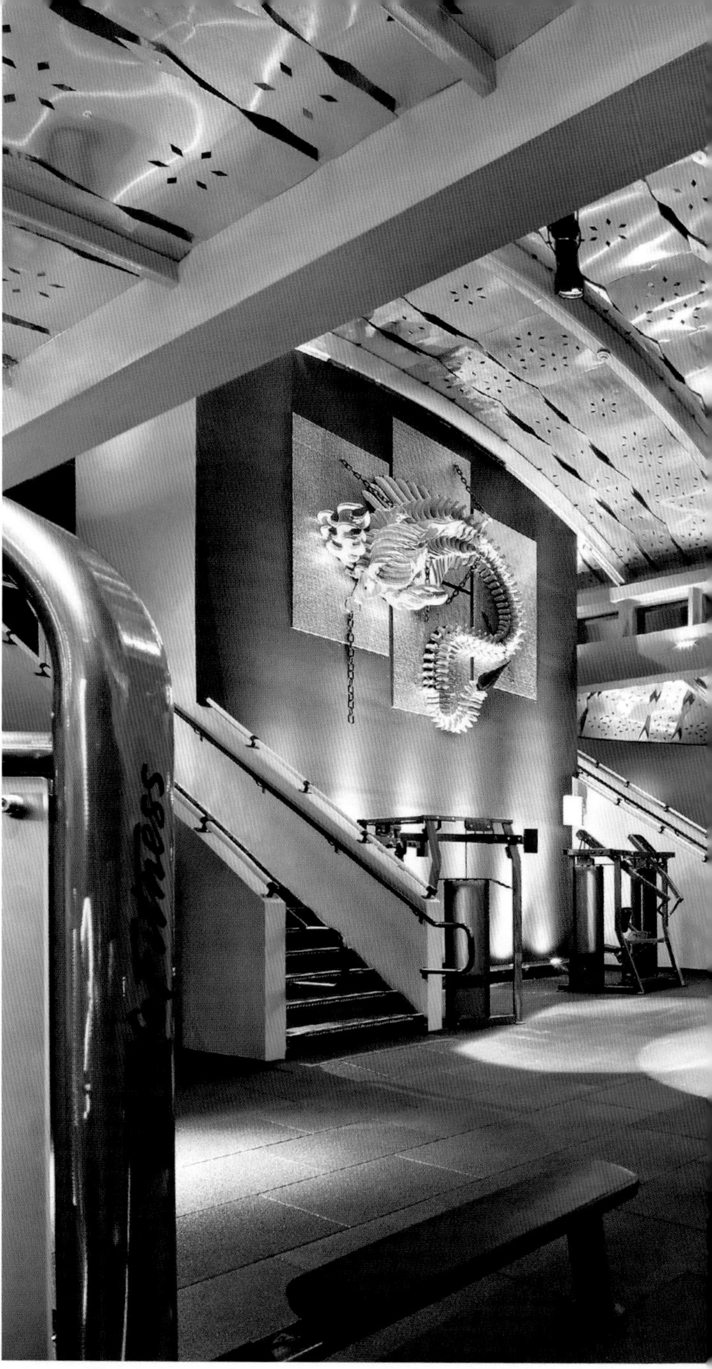

This **club**, one of the **largest gyms** in Florida, **captures** the visitor with its **African charm** and **magically** illuminated pools

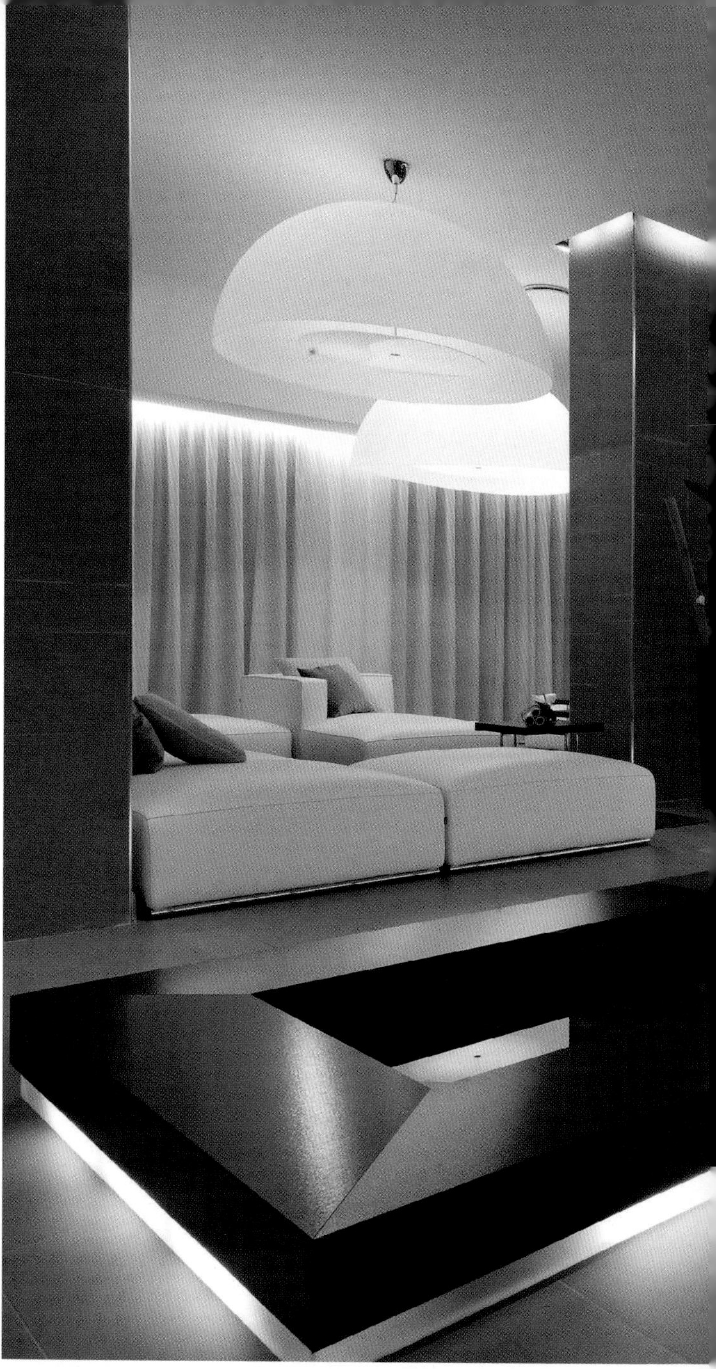

Natural materials like stone, **ceramics,** wood and **leather** were used, **combined** with paths of water and **light**

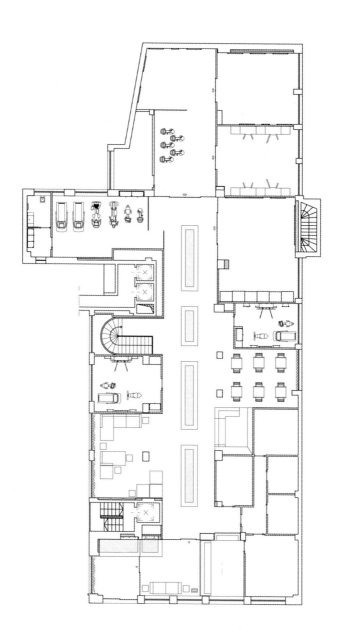

The **combination** of **modern** architecture and the characteristic **Asian** **simplicity** creates a **special** ambiance

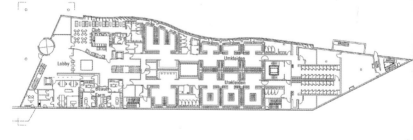

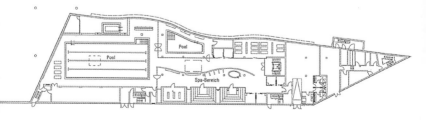

Heartcore Fitness | London | Jess Schuring

The **refurbishment** of the location included the preservation of **original parts** such as **cast iron** beams, **brick walls**, wooden floors

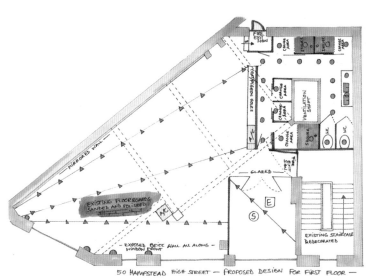

50 HAMPSTEAD HIGH STREET — PROPOSED DESIGN FOR FIRST FLOOR —

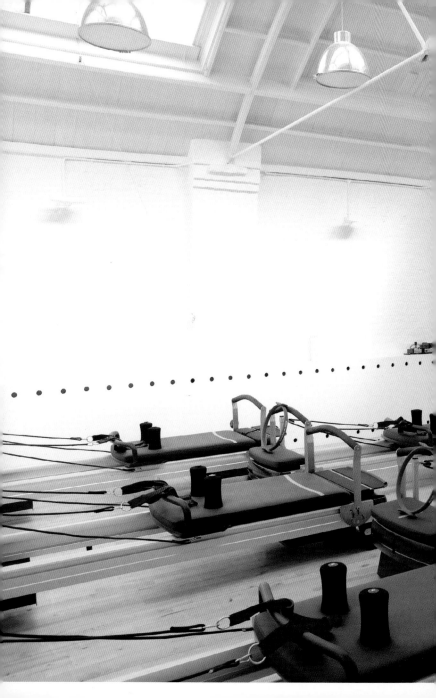

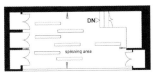

spinning area

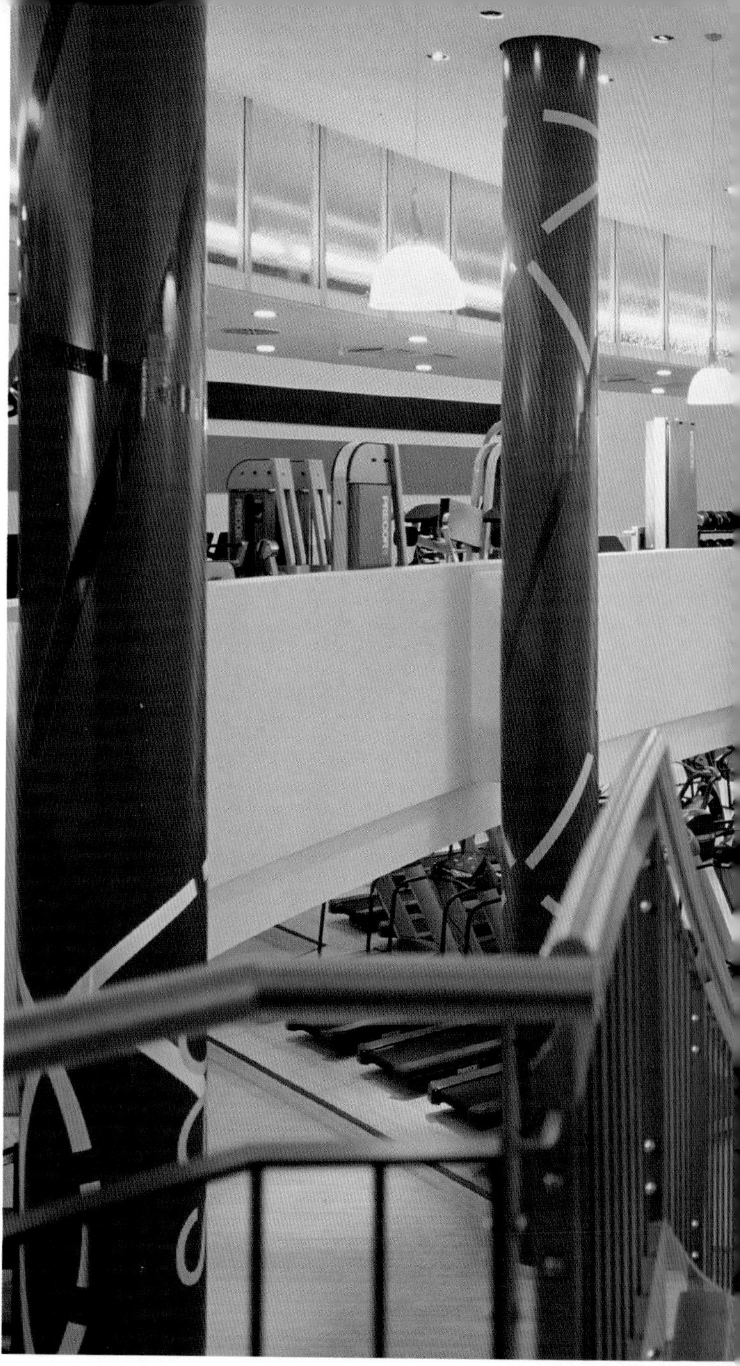

The **dynamic art** concept of the columns **connects** the ground floor with the **upper level**

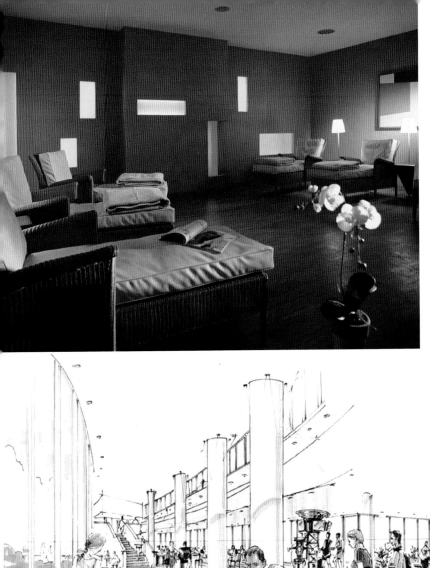

Ibex House / The Strand Holmes Place | London | ORMS Architecture Design

Glass is used extensively to provide insights and to ensure a visual connection throughout

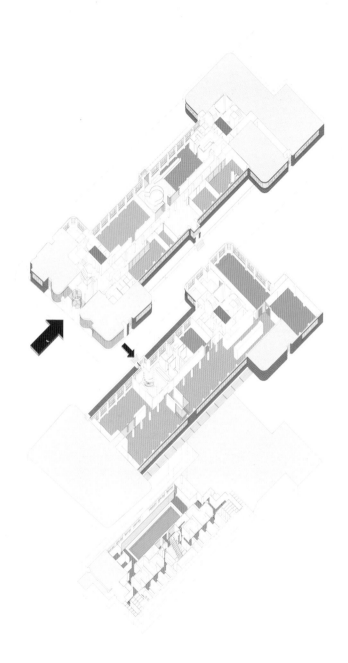

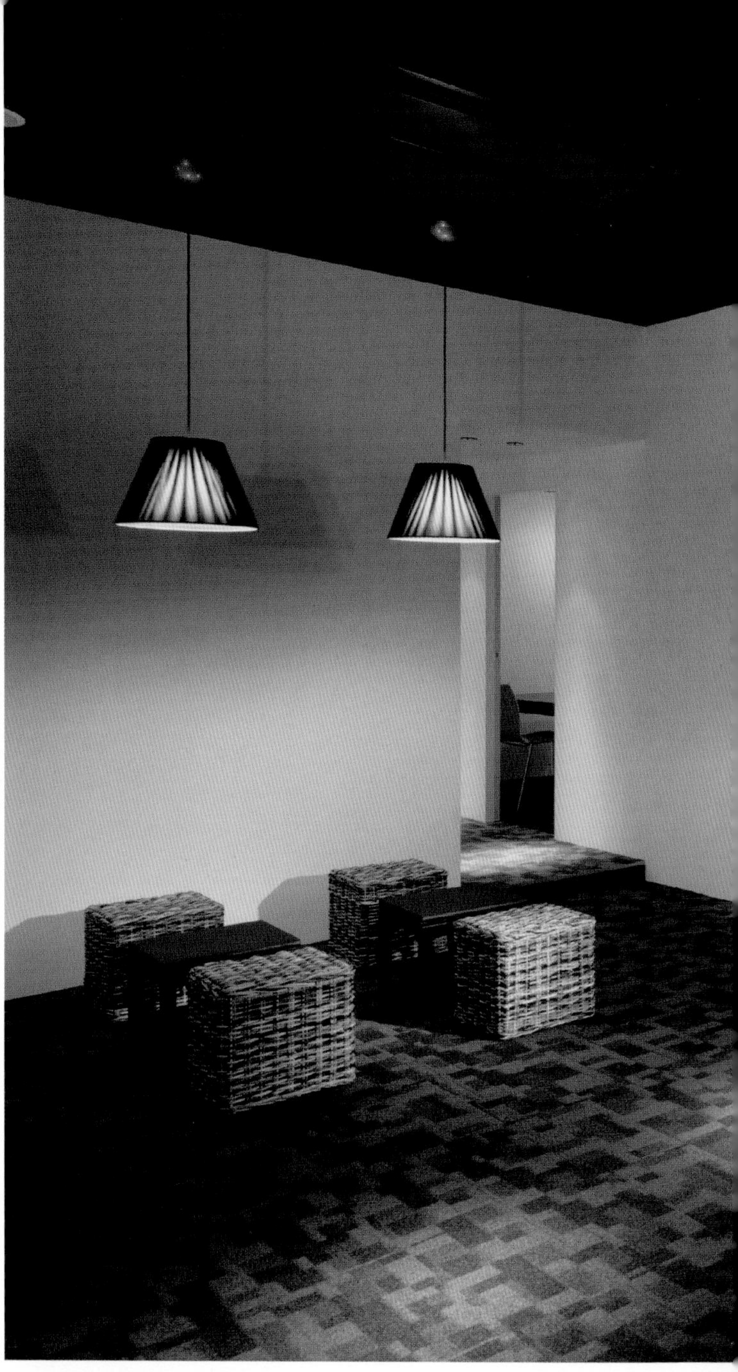

Gold was chosen as key color; a golden rectangle served as the basis for all of the graphics

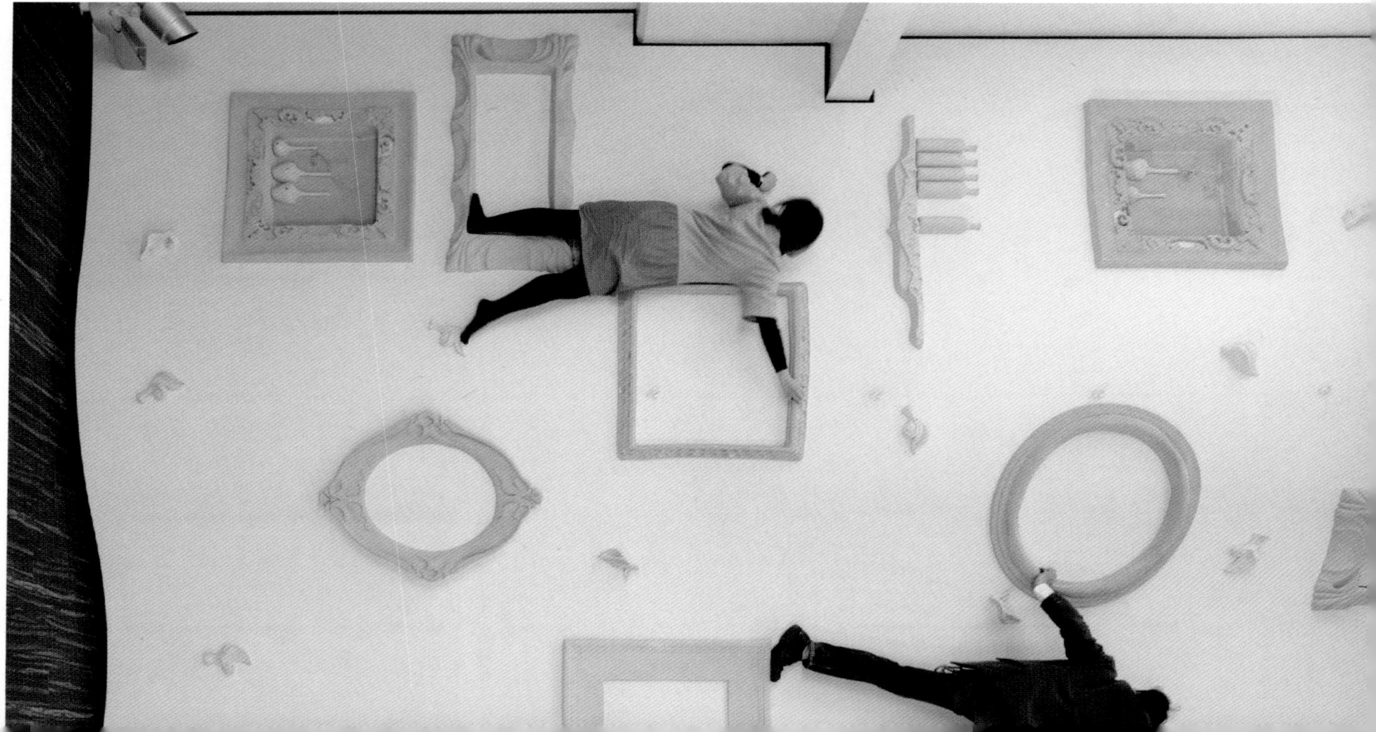

Interior design **elements** were used to create a **challenging climbing** wall

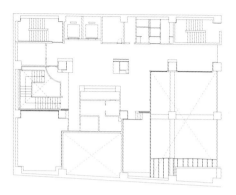

| **Innsbruck Holmes Place Lifestyle Club** | Innsbruck | SEHW Architekten

Warm colors and **strict** geometric **modernity** – define the **design** of this Austrian **fitness** club

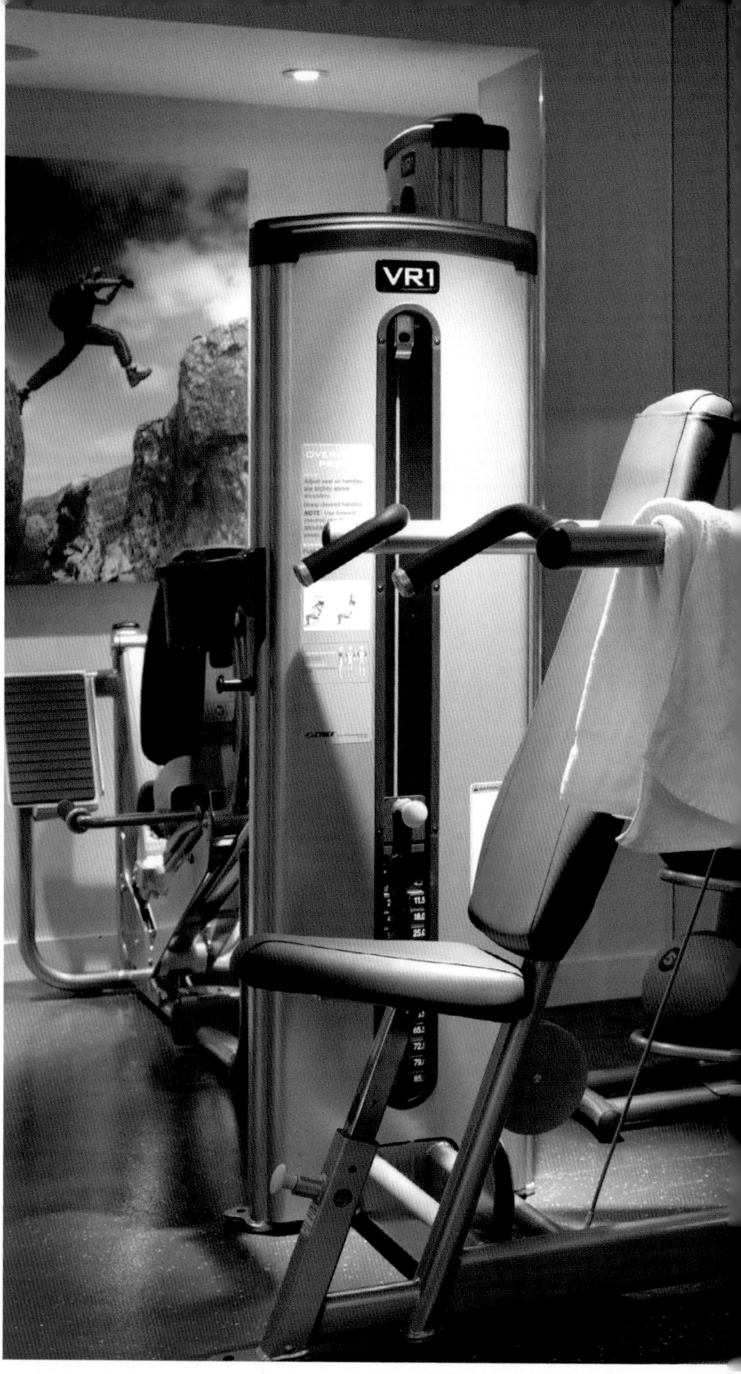

Indigo Fitness Center | London | London Town Hotel ltd.

This **hip hotel gym** echoes **well-being** with its **inspiring** design and **quality equipment**

L'Usine Club de Sport | Geneva | Strausak Associes

This **chic** sports club offers a **variety** of equipment and **services** in a **unique** architectural **surrounding**

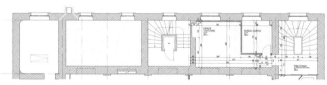

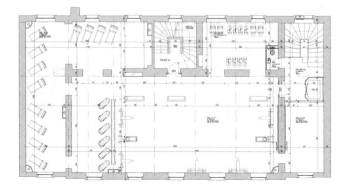

The **clubs** are **designed** to provide **luxurious,** inspirational **training** environments

Design features include a **double-height** gym area traversed by a **raw steel bridge** and a highly atmospheric **black 'batcave'** pool area

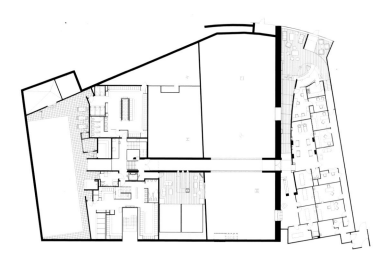

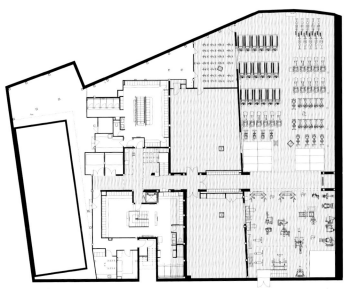

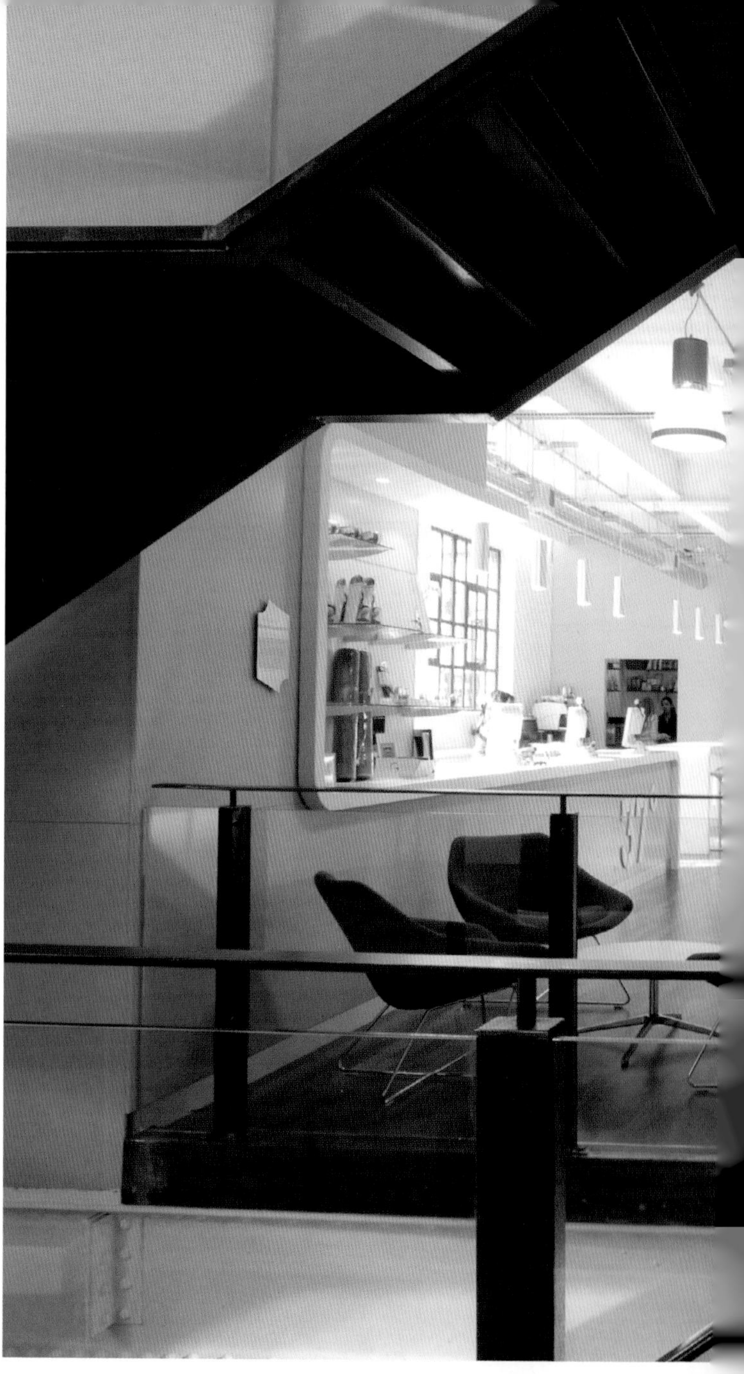

The **center** is **flooded** with **natural light**

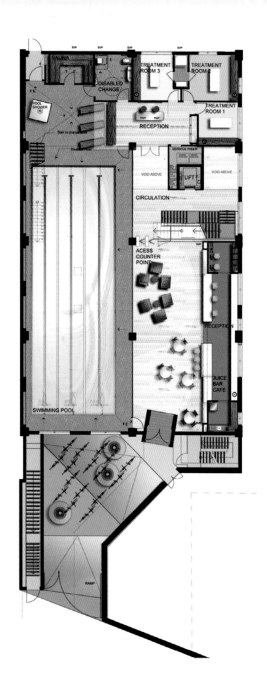

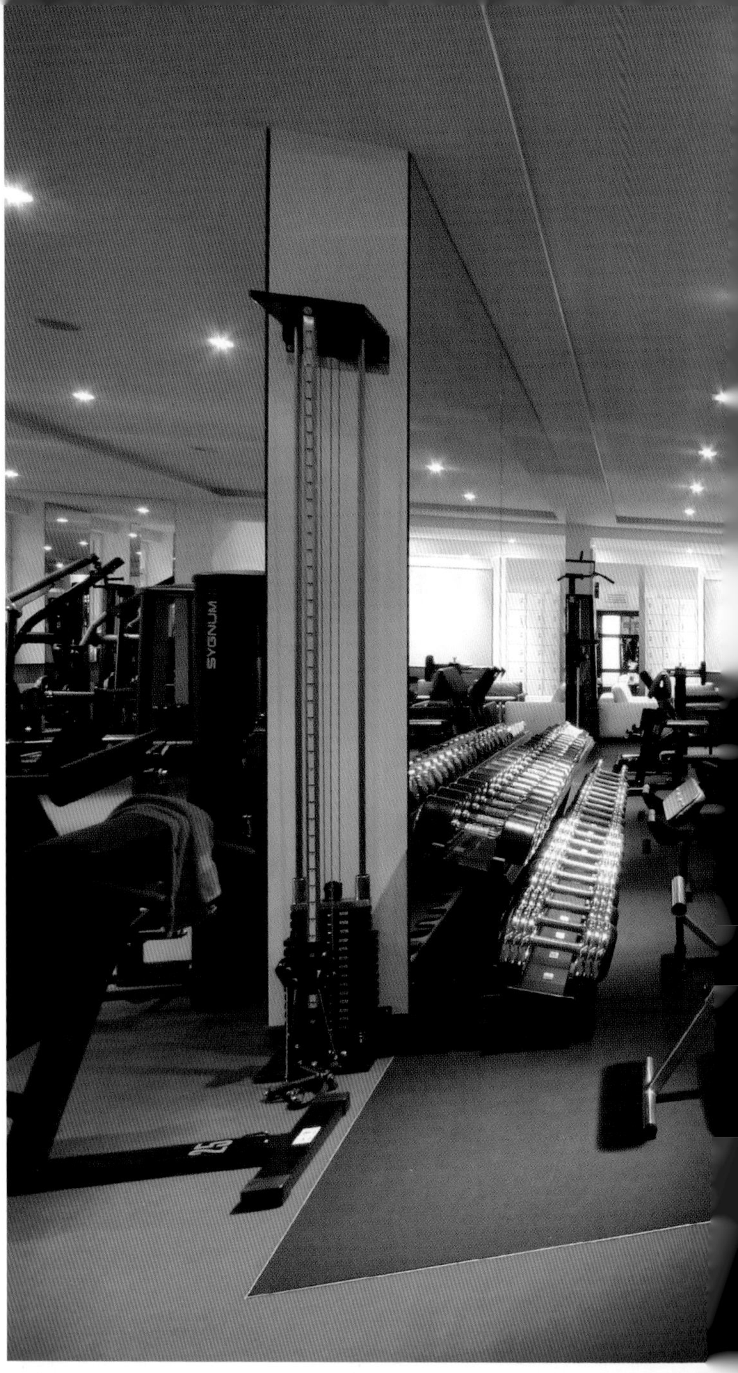
SYGNUM

Red carpet, chrome elements and **black equipment** generate a **posh** ambiance

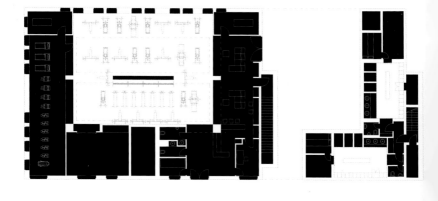

Park Hyatt Istanbul Maçka Palas | Istanbul | Gerner Kronick + Valcarcel, Architects, PC

Elegant teak panels suggest tranquility in the SPA, while metal and glass manifest vigor and vitality in the gym

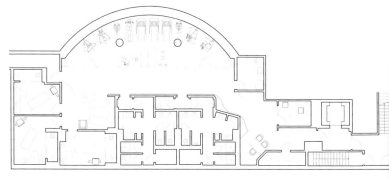

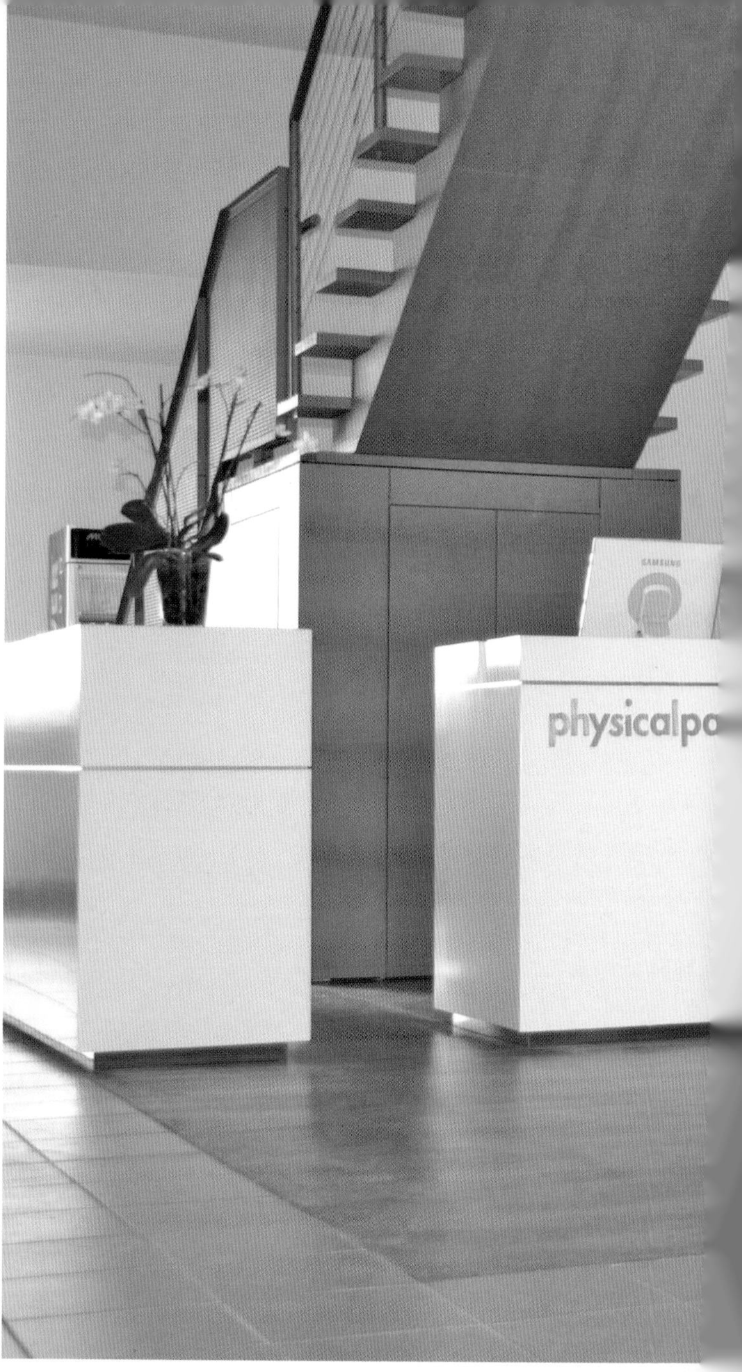

The **welcoming** atmosphere
was **designed** to make
the **guests** feel **comfortable**
and while allowing them to **reach**
their **objectives**

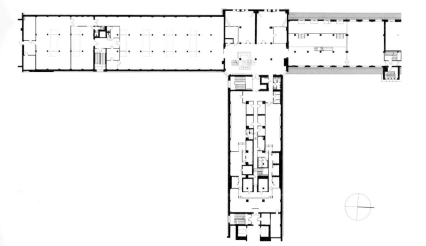

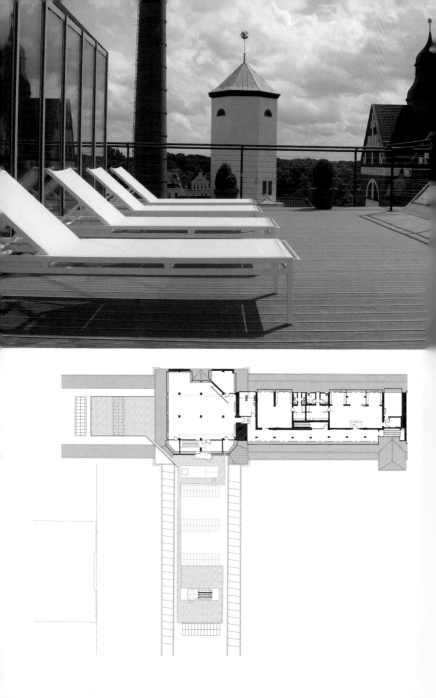

Premium Fitness Club of the Bath Center "Fildorado" | Filderstadt-Bonlanden | Kauffmann Theilig & Partner

Indoor and outdoor ar along a stretched façade which opens to the scenic landscape

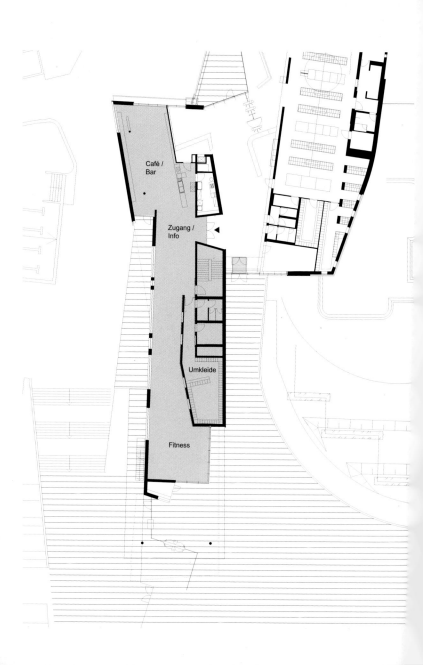

Café /
Bar

Zugang /
Info

Umkleide

Fitness

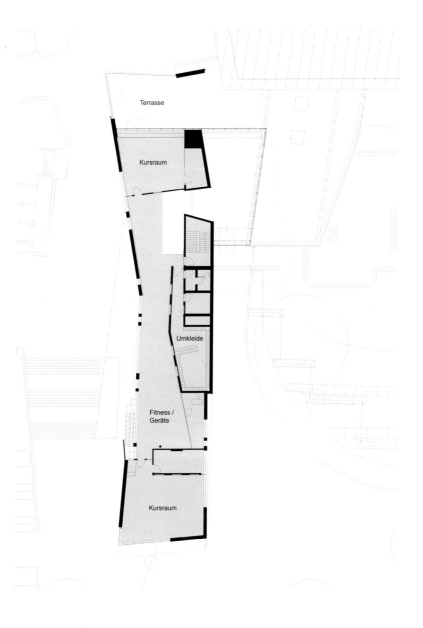

Terrasse

Kursraum

Umkleide

Fitness /
Geräte

Kursraum

The open, **light-flooded** fitness area is **located** in a **landmarked building**

Puls 5 Fitnesspark | Zurich | Oberholzer + Brüschweiler Architekten, Küssnacht | ushitamborriello, Innenarchitektur & Szenenbild, Munich

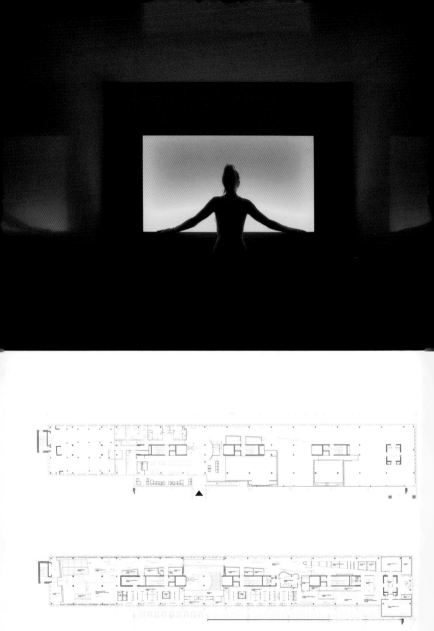

Qi Sport Center | Mexico City | JSª / Javier Sánchez, Jorge Ambrosi, Mariana Pani, Jorge Mdahuar (interior design)

This gym **meets** the needs with regard to **technology** and **comfort,** while being **adapted** to the **style** of the neighborhood

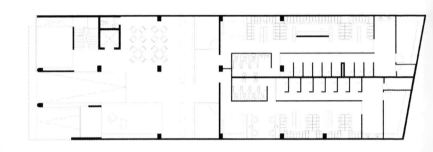

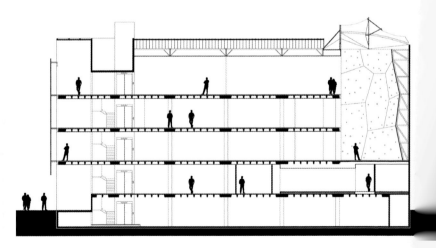

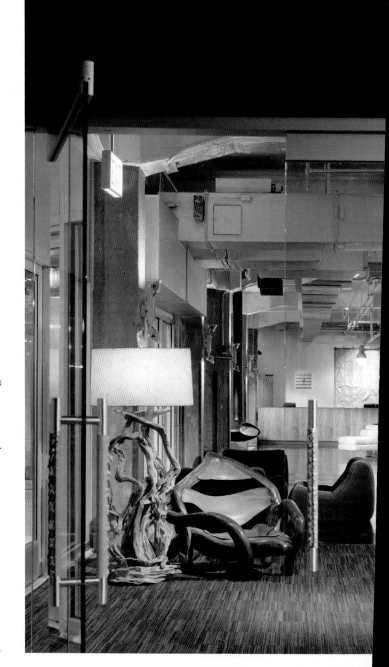

River North DavidBartonGym | Chicago | David Barton

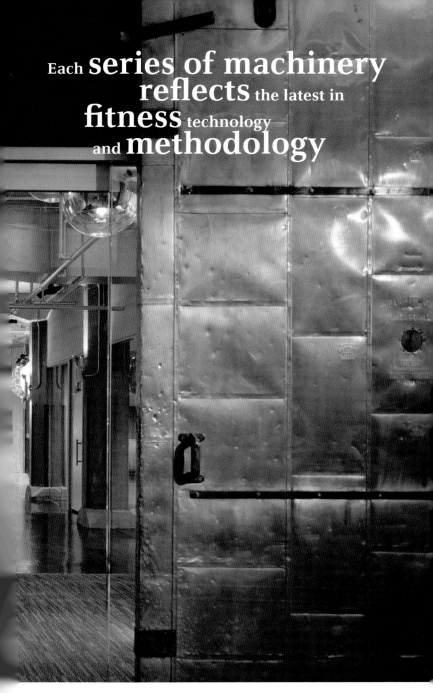

Each **series of machinery reflects** the latest in **fitness** technology and **methodology**

RPM Health Club | Phuket | Sports Engineering and Recreation Asia Ltd.

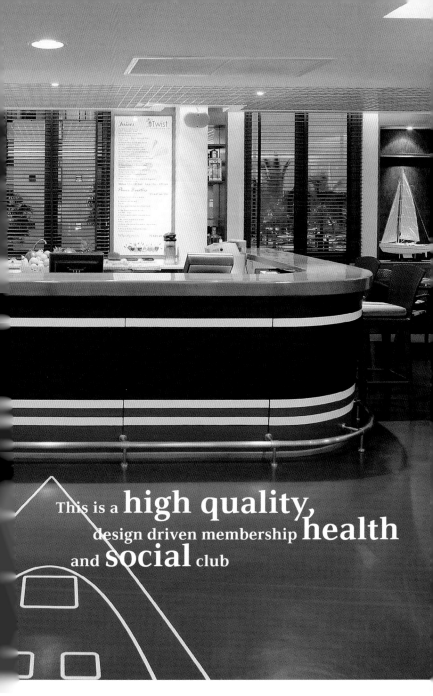

This is a **high quality,** design driven membership **health** and **social** club

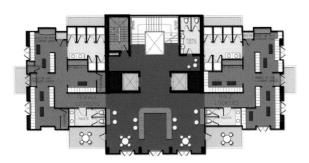

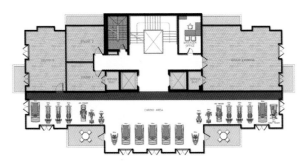

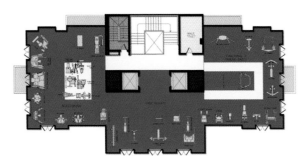

Salzburg Holmes Place Lifestyle Club | Salzburg | SEHW Architekten

Located on **three floors,** the **health** club offers a **combination** of **fitness** and wellness

profile 1

the

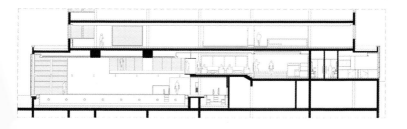

The Spa & **Health Club** features **oriental decor** and ambiance, **radiating** a **magic** charm

Sportstudio Vitarium | Berlin | wiewiorra hopp architekten

Transparent and translucent glass walls create outlines and tension

stretch

The **exercise areas** are
designed to extend
the **panorama** in a layered,
boundless **space**

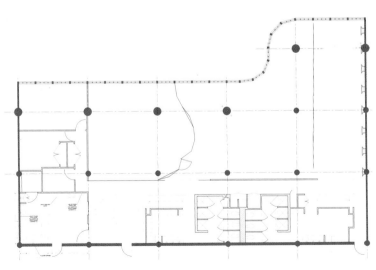

The **overriding** concept of the club **is one** of complete **transparency**

thethirdspace

Images of athletes function as motivation to use the equipment and to get in shape

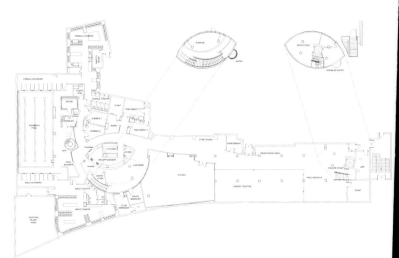

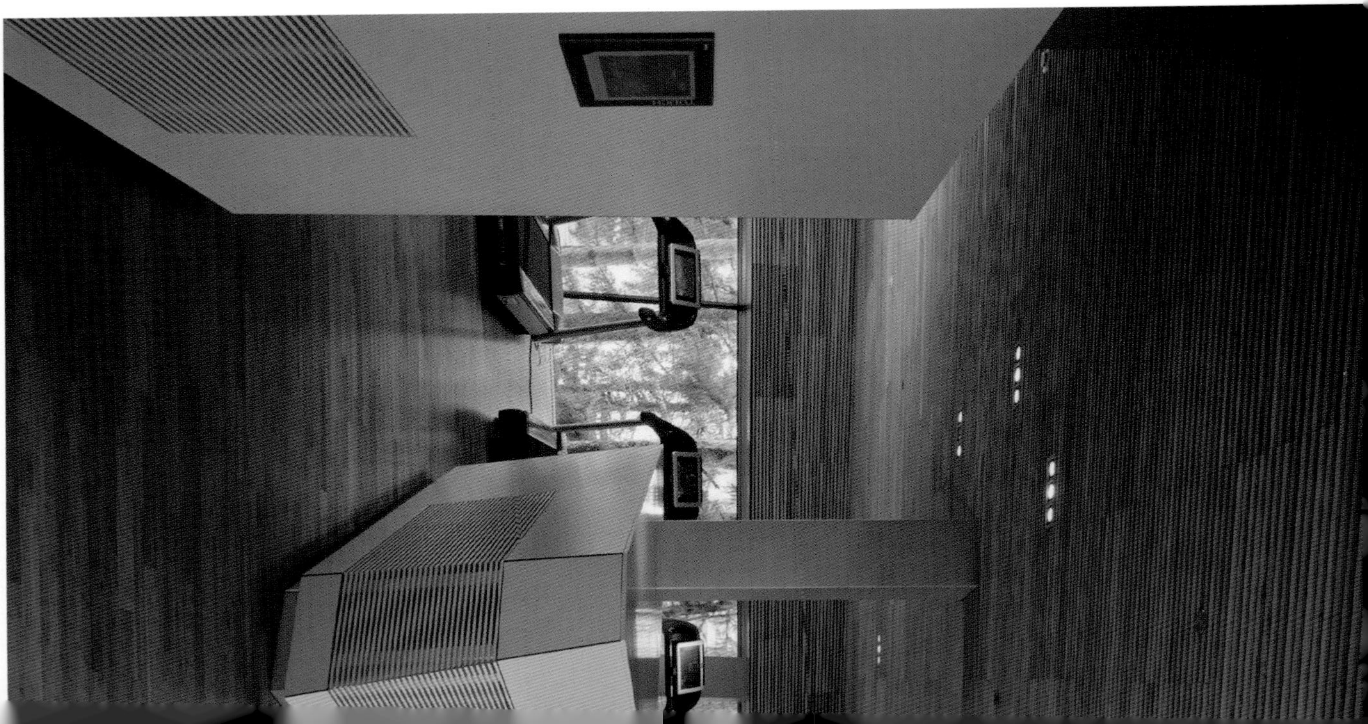

The **construction** of a
recreational landscape
in the **base** of a
residential **high-rise block**

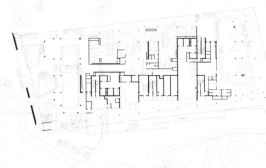

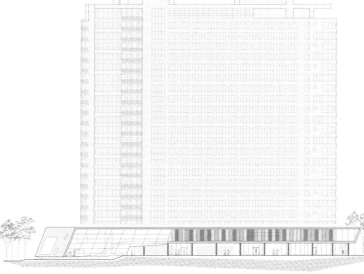

Architects Index

Picture Credits

Ano, Daici	206-213
Balmat, Daniel	226-235
Bildwerk Jochen Splett, Munich	
	298-307
f-com	290-297
Fogelson, Douglas, New York	
	96-105
Gordoa, Luis, Mexico City	308-315
Halbe, Roland	293
HPHC Ibex / London	190-197
Huibers, Ewout	106-119
Klapsch, Thorsten	352-359
KROST, Moscow	388-397
Miralles, Jordi	360-367
Moog, Marco, Hamburg	184-189
Nagaishi, Hidehiko	62-73
O'Callahan, Michael	120-127
SEHW Schreiber Egger Horlitz	
Winkler Hamburg Berlin	
	170-175, 214-221, 334-339

All other photos were made availble
by the architectural firms or
fitness studios.

Cover: Aspria Spa + Sporting Club +
Hotel Berlin